Billy Gets Talking
A Preschooler's Journey Overcoming Childhood Apraxia of Speech

Written and Illustrated by Mehreen Kakwan, M.A., CCC-SLP

Mehreen Kakwan LLC
Ann Arbor, MI

Dedicated to Sydney, Hayden, Jaxon,
Ruby, and Shak with love.

I send gratitude to Lorena for her insight
about colors, expressions, and depth.
I send gratitude to Veena for reviewing every
draft and for her recognition of rhythm.

ISBN: 9781728705163

Billy had a lot
to talk about.
He loved cats.

He loved bath time.

and catching bugs.

He loved
ice cream.

He loved to
listen to stories.

Billy was smart and good at lots of things.

But talking was tricky.

It was hard to say the words in his head.

It was hard to move his mouth how he wanted.

This made Billy feel sad.

Sometimes he felt mad or upset that he was not understood.

So Mommy and Daddy took Billy to meet a new friend.

Billy had fun with his new friend, his Speech language pathologist.

They made silly faces.

They played with toys and games.

They made sounds and he practiced moving his mouth lips and tongue .

Moo!

Mmmooo

Go Billy! His words were getting clearer.

Billy tried his best everyday.
It took time and hard work.
Billy did <u>not</u> give up!

Billy's family helped him practice the movements by showing him signs (cues) along with his sounds.

Mommy asked

Billy said

ME!

Who wants ice cream?

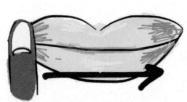 mmmm

 eeee

Daddy asked
Is that a frog?
Billy said
NO!
touch nose
nnn
oh
trace lips

Billy said
Hi!
Granny said
Hi Billy! I love your words my honey bunny
hhh
ah
eeee

After awhile, Billy was talking all the time!

At school, Billy did not feel
shy about talking anymore.

Billy was excited
to talk to his friends.

Billy felt brave enough to speak out in groups.

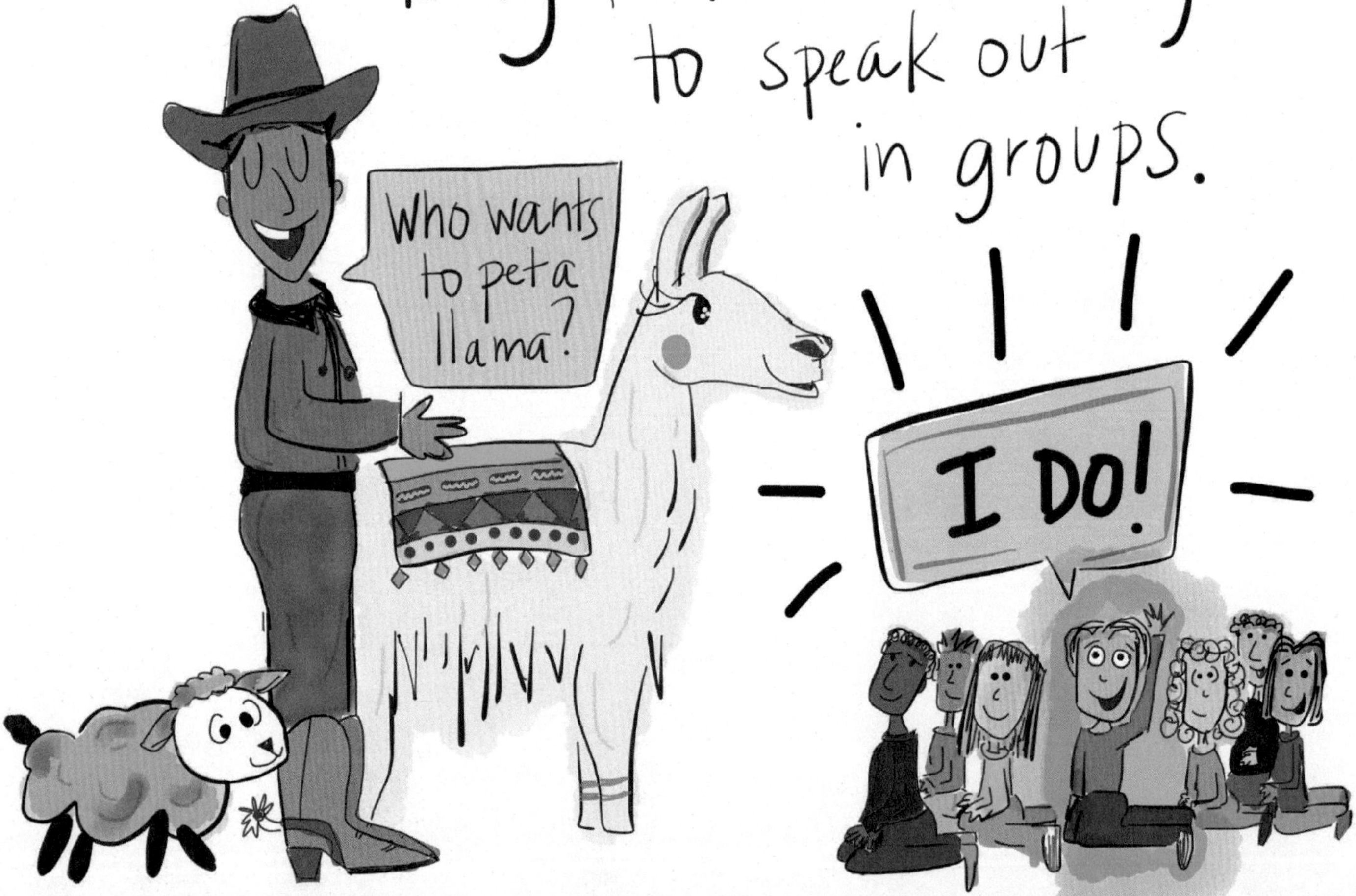

Billy was even easier to understand

He could say
his name now too.

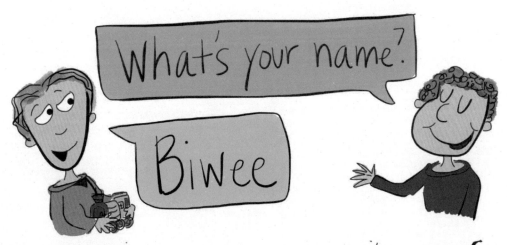

All his sounds were not perfect yet,
and that was okay!

What mattered is that he kept trying his best.

Billy was proud of himself.
It became easier
to move his
mouth to make
his sounds and
words.
Billy felt
understood.

His mommy and daddy were proud of him too.

This all made Billy feel very...

Very...

HAPPY!

AFTERWORD

This children's story focused on Billy's journey to finding his words so he could express himself and fully engage with the world; however, it is also symbolic of the journey many of us grown-ups choose to take when we speak and act in ways that expresses our most authentic selves. Such choices invite a life that resonates most deeply with our highest and best selves. May every heart be healed and graced with the courage to let frustrations of the past and out-dated self-limiting beliefs go, to allow guidance to arrive, to be kind to ourselves when challenges surface, and to embrace the life and Higher Love that is waiting for all of us. We are a series of transformations, each metamorphosis bringing us closer to our true selves.

Childhood Apraxia of Speech (CAS)

CAS is a speech sound disorder characterized by specific difficulty programming oral motor movements for the production of speech sounds. Children with this diagnosis have difficulty coordinating the jaw, lips, and tongue to consistently produce specific speech sounds at the sound, syllable, word, and/or phrase level, depending on severity.

Although ASHA (American Speech-Language and Hearing Association) designates the definition of CAS to ages 3-21, speech-language treatment for CAS may begin by approximately 18 months to 2 years of age, depending on the child. It is recommended that caregivers seek a full speech and language evaluation if they notice their child is demonstrating fewer words compared to same-age peers, reduced intelligibility, and/or frustration due to not being understood.

Internet Resources

www.asha.org/public/speech/disorders/childhood-apraxia-of-speech/
www.apraxia-kids.org
www.slpmommyofapraxia.com

For more information and resources, please visit www.MehreenKakwan.com

ABOUT THE AUTHOR

Mehreen Kakwan is an ASHA (American Speech-Language and Hearing Association) certified speech-language pathologist with a passion for being a catalyst for positive growth and healing. She earned her Master's in Speech-Language Pathology at Eastern Michigan University, and her Bachelor's of Science in Economics and Pre-med at The University of Michigan - Ann Arbor. Inspired by her patient's healing journeys, she combined her love for illustrating and writing with her desire to help more children feel a sense of belonging, self-acceptance and hope.
Mehreen lives in Ann Arbor, Michigan.

Photo by Katelyn Wollet | www.katelynwollet.com

34847838R00018

Made in the USA
Columbia, SC
17 November 2018